Enter the Gateway

A Collection of Christian Poetry

Published by TL Publishing Group

Enter the Gateway © 2013 by TL Publishing Group

Original cover art © James Steidl

Cover art design by © Alice Shantel Saunders

Edited by Alice Saunders and Aisha McFadden

Published by TL Publishing Group

All rights reserved. Except for use of brief quotations in any review, the reproduction of this work in whole or in part in any form is forbidden without the prior written permission of TL Publishing Group.

ISSN- 10: 0615783570
ISBN-13: 978-0615783574

Ordering Information:
Visit http://shop.torridliterature.com to order copies

TL Publishing Group
www.torridliterature.com

Dedication

To His Children, both lost and found.

Table of Contents

Jane Blanchard

Re: Paul to Timothy	1
Invigoration	2
Pass It On	3

Audrey Williams

Church	4

Lisbon Tawanda Chigwenjere

Days of My Youth	7
The Tongue of the Learned	8
Fight, Soldier, Fight	9

Thomas Koron

The Gates of Paradise	10

Erren Geraud Kelly

The Light of Protection (Psalms 91)	11
Answered Prayers	12
6 Weeks	14
A New Wig	15

Oneal Walters

When to Pray	16

Makeba Jackson

The Powerful Pen	17
Use Me	18
The Wedding Vows	19
Bring the Rain	20
Christy's Melody	21
Don't Pass It Up	22
Place of Peace	23

Richard Hartwell

Early Flight	24
Safe Harbor	25
Feral Fog	26
Prey	27

David Schildroth

Intervention	28

Cathy Baker

The One	30

Carol Meeks

Angels Help Drop God's Paintbrush	31
Before My Birth, He Knew Me	32
As Lad, King David Ran From Saul	33

Nels Hanson

The Question That Was Never Asked	34
The Mourning Dove Recalls a Place	36
Sir Knight	38

Marchell Dyon Jefferson

Born on a Sunday	39
Sevenling (A Daughter's Psalm)	40

Michael Miller

Victory	41

Mark Nenadov

They Laughed At Him	44
Breath by Breath	45

Jesse Chandler

Evensong LXXX: Words in an Empty Shell	46
Evensong XIV: Watch on the Water	47

"Through Him also we have [our] access (entrance, introduction) by faith into this grace (state of God's favor) in which we [firmly and safely] stand. And let us rejoice and exult in our hope of experiencing and enjoying the glory of God."

Romans 5:2 AMP

Re: Paul to Timothy
(2 Timothy 4:3-4)

Heeding truth is hard to do,
As the test of time makes clear;
Doctrine sounds, but very few
Listen to what they should hear.
Myth is so appealing to
Those who want to scratch an ear;
When desire does itch anew,
Fools seek fools from far and near.

Author: Jane Blanchard

Invigoration

The Sistine painter understood so well
The bond between divinity and man.
It is amazing how a fresco can
Portray in splendor what mere words but tell
In truth. Beneath Creation, I am spell-
bound as I lean to look upon the span
Of arms extended to fulfill God's plan
For one designed to stand until two fell.

As God drew Adam out of primal dust,
He pulls man still from mires of sin and strife
To walk, to work, to rest on higher ground.
Faith stretched to reach's length develops trust
That Maker's strength can sanctify each life.
Through touch is grace bestowed and blessing found.

Author: Jane Blanchard

Pass It On

As legend goes, the dogwood tree
was cut for use at Calvary.

And ever since that crucial date
it tries to grow more bent than straight.

Its flower, though, of petals four
looks like the cross it forms no more.

Each one is notched, and tinted, too,
as if wounds left both hole and hue.

But each one does its best to hold
a crown of what surpasses gold.

For seeds soon fall upon the ground
and spread the legend all around.

Author: Jane Blanchard

Church

White store-front building
stained glass windows
deep dark red mahogany rug
the sanctuary that made you feel protected
open hearts and minds
angels in white gloves
praying hands
announcements
the Lord's words
sitting in the bench pew familiar wood
intense tingly feelings traveling through me

the microphone
Reverend Sammy Lewis speaking from the pulpit
eloquent sermons
the Bible
pastor's gold ice pitcher and glass
chinking ice
HIS words are alive
HIS body, crumbled pieces of dry crackers
HIS blood, red grape juice in tiny cups
my spirit, soaring free

the choir loft
the upright organ
standing and clapping
singing The Lord Will Make A Way praises
shouting and jumping as the mood strikes
bringing the congregation to its feet
strong and powerful voices touch all
Feeling the Holy Ghost
Miss Ella threw her handkerchief every time
testifying
witness

opening the doors of the church

walking down the aisle
my second home
the Lord lives
peace that surpasses all understanding
shepherds
stewardship

the altar cloth
tambourines
Sunday best
those not so blest
uppity ones
opened arms
down and out looking for the light
loving family
worshipping the Lord
weeping eyes
joyful heart
mother board,
missionary board
outreach
building fund
offering envelopes
pastor love offering
flowing dresses,
robes navy blue and white
ties or open collared shirts
Sunday shoes
people dressed in
red, blue, purple, yellow and green
brown, black, golden, white

Sunday dinners
the small open hall
the bright yellow walls
white aprons
pungent smells
golden fried chicken

red spaghetti trails
white potato salad
and corn bread

feeling loved, sheltered,
wanted and needed
church family.

Author: Audrey Williams

Days of My Youth

I once preached to a man in a telephone booth
Long ago during the days of my youth
I grew up different from the other boys
As a little boy I studied the scriptures and avoided toys

When I was past being a child
I did not care whether it was hot, cold or mild
I travelled seventy-four kilometers to preach in Marandellas;
Now my dream goes even beyond Dallas

I was a teenager then;
But I could invade a lion's den
I was so strong and bold
I could preach even in the cold
During the days of my youth
I remembered my creator

Author: Lisbon Tawanda Chigwenjere

The Tongue of the Learned

When I quarrel my voice reaches to the South,
Lord, put a cello tape on my mouth,
I want to re-learn speaking,
That's all I am seeking
Like a little child teach me anew,
Teach me words I never knew,
Your Word I want to treasure,
So that in my words you will find pleasure

Author: Lisbon Tawanda Chigwenjere

Fight, Soldier, Fight

"Thou therefore, endure hardness, as a good soldier of Jesus Christ."
(2 Timothy 2:3)

Stand in the victory that Christ has won,
For all of us, not for one,
Be strong, soldier, be strong,
In the end you shall sing a victory song
You are the heir of the monarch of the universe
It's clearly revealed in David's verse,
Your Father is rich, soldier; your father is God,
He is the owner of silver and gold
At the end we shall have a heavenly feast,
But while on earth fight not with your fists,
We wrestle not against flesh and blood,
Your back up will come like a flood,
Fight, soldier, fight
Whatever opposition comes in sight
As a good soldier endure hardship,
In the midst of hardship praise and worship,
This is the will of God, soldier, this is what He wills
Your enemies will flee at the sound of Chariot wheels
Health for us did His pain yield,
By Christ's wounds you were truly healed,
Refuse to be sick, soldier; refuse!
Your body is not for the devil's misuse
Stand in the victory that Christ has won,
For all of us, not for one,
Be strong, soldier, be strong,
In the end you shall sing a victory song

Author: Lisbon Tawanda Chigwenjere

The Gates of Paradise

There reaches a point within our lives where
We all long for some comfort from our grief.
A sense of mercy and welcoming care;
Rewards for our devotion and belief.
Witnessing the glory of heaven and
The peace we feel while standing at the gates.
Cherishing the warmth of His healing hand,
With the feeling that paradise awaits.
Holiness returns us to our freedom;
All pain is gone, and joyfulness abounds.
We're cleansed upon entering His kingdom,
As we rest peacefully above the clouds.
He brings an end to suffering and loss;
To save mankind, He died upon the cross.

Author: Thomas Koron

The Light of Protection (Psalms 91)

doctors could play god
if they wanted to
sometimes, they even let robots
operate
my mama told me

she undressed put on a robe
and lie on a table and a light
surrounded her as if
god put his shield of protection
around her to let
everyone know
she belonged to
him

the light surrounded her
and the light didn't become flames
and the light didn't let anyone
near her

the light was god
and it kept all evil spirits
at bay
just as it did the night
someone kicked her door in
and tried to rob her

the light surrounded her
and drove the evil spirit away
just as it will do
every time she lie on
the radiation table

Author: Erren Geraud Kelly

Answered Prayers

i made a deal with god

if he healed my mother
i would get closer to him
i don't think i'll have a
problem keeping it

the world doesn't give me much
to believe in anymore
writing is important to me
but it's not the most
important thing
i love women, but they're
not the most important thing
either
god has healed my mother
the doctor told her the
cancer is gone
she gets the clean slate
others long for
another chance to get it
right
so, i don't care what happens to me
now
i don't care what people
think of me
not that i ever did
i'm just happy to be here
happy that there is a tomorrow
for her
and no matter how many times i
get published or rejected
it won't matter
it is good to have a
tomorrow
to know that you live another

day to be thankful
and i am thankful to god
for saving my mother
and i grateful to god
for giving me the will and the strength
to write
and i am grateful to god
for saving anyone else
who deserves
someone once told me
" god is an on-time god..."
that he comes to you in the
nick of time
not when you want him
but when he wants to
god is an on-time god...
my mother says
who never doubted she
would be healed
who always believed
she would win
i made a deal with god

i'm going to keep it

yet

Author: Erren Geraud Kelly

6 Weeks

42 days...
that's how long mama's got to wait
until her next doctor's appointment
it's the equivalent
of a man on death row
waiting for word from the governor
to see if his stay of execution
went through
it's like checking my mail from publishers
hoping my work was
accepted

someone told me time moves faster
when you're not watching it

a few weeks ago
mama cooked for the first time
since the surgery
i told her just ease back
into life
because it's the same today
as it was yesterday

each day she moves closer and closer
to paradise....

Author: Erren Geraud Kelly

A New Wig

preferably brunette
though she would work as a redhead
she'll wear it so it covers her head
completely
so her potential man won't notice
but he won't care
every day for one month
she entered the radiation machine
to be born again
she never had a a doubt
60 years of being a christian
would see her through
no one says anything
about her hair falling out
they're just glad she's still here
sometimes, she wears a bandanna
and the people in the neighborhood
say she's hip

but she just smiles and sits
in her backyard

Author: Erren Geraud Kelly

When to Pray

My God, Yahweh
humble be your chosen ones;
set us free from debt, oppression
and surrounding enemies.
Bad health flees at your will,
our bodies are flawed here on earth.
Forgive us! Our sins are many from birth.
Build your family so we rely not on strangers.
Create life; always bless us with sons and daughters.
Show your light, continually guiding us with your hand.
Rich and poor, you designed this, we understand.
We labor to build on your foundation;
in due season, you are the reason for prosperity.
You are faithful,
thank you.

Author: Oneal Walters

The Powerful Pen

Father what can I write for you
A melody so sweet
Maybe a story telling how I overcame defeat
Explaining my victory, my triumph over despair
Telling you the history as if you weren't there
My mind is full of ideas just waiting to be expressed
Give me a pen a paper
On it I will caress: thoughts and feelings, stemming
From the human intellect
I recognize my ideas their worth and all that they hold
The potential to shape, the power of people's souls
So Father continue to direct this pen changing the hearts of men
Transforming these words to be used like an instrument
Oh God the glory you'll receive for inspiring people like me

Author: Makeba Jackson

Use Me

Take my hand you're full of fire
Mold me, shape me
I'm yours to brand
Use me according to your command
I'm your vessel your work of clay
Heated in a form forced to stay
Broken and burned no longer mottled clay
Ready for your work of art
I'm your canvas paint on me
Use me as a tool for your glory
Set aside for your purpose to accomplish your plan
Lord I'm yours to do your will as you demand
Lord use me for your purpose, your plan
Lord use me
I want to meet your demands your work of art
Your jar of clay
Your earthen vessel forced to stay in a mold you made
Lord you can use me

Author: Makeba Jackson

The Wedding Vows

This is my vow to you a heart felt cry
As I stand before man viewing you through God's eyes
I pray that he keeps me steadfast and true
For it's only through him that I can do what I do
All things are possible be assured
It's only through Christ our love will endure
I promise to look to heaven where my strength comes from
To fulfill my wifely duties just like the Proverbs 31:10 woman
It is my plea to you
I hope you will comply
Let us live the life that God has designed
I will honor, cherish and respect you as long as we both live
Luis I love you.
Never forget
Lord bind our hearts and minds together as one
Fill us with your spirit from this time forth and forever to come

Author: Makeba Jackson

Bring the Rain

One single night I spent searching for rain
Hoping to find peace in my heart again
Joy came and then it left
I said to myself while I wept, "Be encouraged the joy you had before
Will you find you again."
So I wept no more and released the pain
Knowing deep inside nothing is in vain
Weeping may endure for a night but joy comes in the morning
Be strong in the Lord in the power of his might
Hold tight to your faith and you won't loose the fight
Rest in his peace
Be assured
Nothing is without gain in the Father's sight
He knows your pain
Come to the Lord frequently
He implores
Don't ignore
He will bring the rain you've been searching for

Author: Makeba Jackson

Christy's Melody

Christy is a Queen
Making melodies in her head
She thought she'd do other things
Like save the sick or raise the dead
Instead her pencil is her scepter
Her ruling authority is in what she says
Death and life are in the power of the tongue
So Christy has the gift to heal the sick and raise the dead
Little did she know it would be in what she sung or said
Christy is a physician who ministers with her words
Using her melodies to heal the hurt
Resurrect a new goal in the minds of men who thought they would
never dream again
God gives us all different talents and strengths
Christy's is the gift of song
A queen in her own right who makes melodies as she walks along
the path of life
Using her ability to sing, she brings life
Christy is a physician at first she didn't know
Now she recognizes her calling ministering to all who come and go.

Thank God for the talents he's given you he knows what's needed for
balance and harmony to exist in this world

Author: Makeba Jackson

Don't Pass It Up

Do something
Finish it up
When a task is not complete, don't sit around patting your feet
Wondering
Hi ho, fiddle dee dum
I wonder who will get the job done
Will it be me or will I keep the project from reaching full capacity
Take some initiative
Get up
Don't be a fool and pass it up
When opportunity knocks do you say do not enter
Come back when I feel like getting up
NO, you seize the moment
Get some gumption!
Get up!
Don't be a fool and pass it up!

Author: Makeba Jackson

Place of Peace

Safe in your arms
Who can bring such surety
Who can bring such peace
Who can take me to the holy place, that place of sacred peace
My mind often wonders
It's seldom at ease
But there is someone
Who can take me back to his place of sacred peace

Author: Makeba Jackson

Early Flight

I launch my pleas for a brave new day
Into the backyard of my expectant morning.
I encounter there the starry constellations,
Dewdrops scattered across the cobwebs.
Centered in this universe lies the waiting spider
Hungering for the intrepid, the dawn breakers.
She is sly, not sinister or malevolent,
Waiting in a firmament of silken trajectories.
Her patience is infinite and often rewarded
With a periodicity worthy of an immortal.
She is poised, and like me, is awaiting
Vibrations from dies fortis novus.

Author: Richard Hartwell

Safe Harbor

Only the smallest of crystalline white sails
Peeks round the promontory at first,
Then dissipates.
A scout ship I surmise, sent ahead to map the coast,
Plumbing coastal depths of evanescent blue,
In preparation to attack.
By mid-afternoon ships-of-the-line move in beneath the sun,
Out of the northwest, from beneath the horizon,
Steadily mounting on more sail.
Slender, soaring masts of eucalyptus support their billowing advance.
By evening they will jibe away and pop cumulus spinnakers,
Then they will make a final gun-run on the port.
Apocalyptic thunderheads conceal an invading fleet bent on engulfing me each day,
But I know the secret of their defeat rests within the patience of the dark,
When the wind will shift by dawn and blow them out to sea.
When
And
Where,
Scattered by the offshore breezes,
Closed-hauled canvas clouds,
Regrouped by noon,
Will come about,
And assault
Us once
Again.

Author: Richard Hartwell

Feral Fog

Feral fog on the south coast of Oregon
Insinuates itself into the core of the girl,
Subversively seeking entrance to the soul,
Shredding memories in the mists of mind.
She drives again those roads past years of
Reflection before being blinded by a flash:
Oncoming lights of another night escapee.

Verifiable truth of feral fog south of Coos Bay
Lies not in the slow cat's crawl over the North Coast,
Not as a wall of white waste folding itself
Across the Golden Gate, into Frisco Bay,
Not like morning smoke of spring in lower California,
Inadequately arresting momentary attention. An
Untamed truth clings to her; no returning home.

The feral fog envelops the night,
Sealing off escape from littered thoughts,
Stamping for her attention on this drive.
Shrouds of personal ambition pull aside,
Awaiting veils of misunderstanding to lift,
Revealing new directions, new destinations,
Reversing exposure of her self-sequestering.

Author: Richard Hartwell

Prey

I saw an old friend today –

Sighted in the mirror of my drawn face,
Marked with the lines of despair,
Focused, drawn into dappled shadows.

How many times have I been chased?
By whom? to where? and why? and,
By-and-by, was I ever caught? and,
What became of me?
Was I captured? slyly poached? or,
Trophy-hunted to extinction?

Questions squeezed in
Before the cross-hairs
Align on the rest of my life.

-- Triggered by the pressure points.

Author: Richard Hartwell

Intervention

In the desert that was my soul
I dwelled on nightly the bell that tolls
Resilient it rang for me at that time
No more lurid sound ever entered my mind

As I lay in my sweat sodden sheets
Taking note of my dwindling heartbeat
This life I have chosen; a dreadful slum
A wretched existence I have become

From the world I need not sympathy
I have taken my actions consciously
The warning from all, I did not heed
As if I knew what in life I need

In silence I ponder what could have been
A life of service away from sin
The boundaries of vision begin to glow
Getting close now; breathing is slow

Eyelids falling with no resistance
To the world I will no longer be a nuisance
No longer tremens, no shakes or headaches
No more judgment for all my mistakes

It's not like I thought. It's not just a game
If given the chance I'd do nothing the same
I failed you Lord there can be no excuse
I've took what you gave me and shown it abuse

I'm evil Lord, I know that I am
I did it my way and cast out the Lamb
I ask for grace but it shouldn't be mine
Please stay with them Lord, the ones who still have time

Finally I know what I could never see

A love for creation; even one like me
I'm so sorry Lord; I'm a disgrace at best
Here I come to you now, a failure of your test

I awake with a jolt in a world so surreal
What treachery awaits; what chilling ordeal?
Oceans of sludge and mountains of dirt
I drop to the ground in endless hurt

Drawing my eyes upwards, reluctantly
A pillar of light forms where it should not be
The ground starts to quake and the air starts to shudder
Wings shoot out of a pearl and gold color

Radiant white blinds my eyes
Brilliance flashes across the dark skies
Judgment has come to the world of despair
I have much to fear if His justice is fair

Divinity above descending to me
Cowardice fails when I want to flee
A large hand extends, weathered and strong
Only I can seize it, I should have known all along

Author: David Schildroth

The One

She steps into her room,
The one doused in lilac,
Letting uncertainty melt into relief.
At her side is security,
Cloaked in cotton, loved—but frayed
Like her.
Beneath the door of her parent's room,
The one where hushed pleas hauntingly loom,
He litters their home with salty sorrow,
Dampening her security, changing its form,
And hers.
Gathering his life in leather that day,
The one wrapped in November's steel gray,
He chooses the scent of a grass greener than his,
Trapping betrayal just beneath the surface
Of her life.
Toward her father, tear-splotched fingers wave,
The one surety she's known, the love he gave.
He saunters past her, toward a new life,
Unraveling threads of every tomorrow.
Not hers alone.
She steps into her life,
The one doused in royalty.
Letting insecurities melt into relief.
At her side is Abba, the One,
Cloaked in perennial grace,
Like her.

Author: Cathy Baker

Angels Help Drop God's Paintbrush

O God. I see an euphony of paint.
The stars ignite dusk's rug!
The moon rock smiles in smug!
The welkin vault slides 'round the earth aglow,
reflects the gold-splashed rings as halo's show
what angels wear. They wear without complaint.
O God. I hear an euphony of paint.
O God. I feel a woven piece of art,
a life-time tapestry,
and Master's ministry
which tempers me in luster's fine like gold.
and gives me strength to join His holy fold.
He cleanses me. He gives a fresh new start.
O God. The textile threads restore my heart.

Author: Carol Meeks

Before My Birth, He Knew Me

Before my birth the Lord knew me---
the hairs on my head, the voice off-key,
and as I grew - the more He knew;
'cause changes gave me footprints' shoe.
I study His word in a quiet place
which strengthens me in mercy's grace.
My thoughts are cleansed by daily reads
and steps directed with holy seeds.
I pray in faith, communion with God---
petition for His spirits' nod,
then hope instills serenity;
and opens God's window, heavenly.
I want to ponder Him as Mary did
so He will keep me from life's skid.
I'm in awe of what He does for me;
His mercy and grace set me free.

Author: Carol Meeks

As Lad, King David Ran From Saul

BALLADE

His fathers' flock, as white as night is tar,
returns at dusk and lies outside his tent
and there he plays his tunes. Each chord a star,
and guides their paths when day's sunlight is spent.
Once, with his Father's blessing and assent,
he brought a giant's bragging to a halt;
adversities were everywhere he went
and yet, when king, he lives for God's exalt.
The young man's name is known in lands afar
for he outshines the evil king's intent
whose threats and jealous rages left their scar.
With lad, the king loves war and won't relent;
but lad, when summoned, plays his psalms in print.
For music soothes Saul's soul like seasoned salt,
and lad forgives this Saul who had to vent
and yet, when king, he lives for God's exalt.
The youth matures above all wisdom's par,
with help from One above, he can repent,
since choices made, hand him a jolt and jar;
mistakes, with age, grow faint - like perfume's scent.
His offspring break his heart in last days spent
and he accepts the things which were his fault,
for he regrets the rules they broke and bent,
and yet, when King, he lives for God's exalt.
Prince, prince from line of Jesus Christ descent
and Jesse's roots, he runs from Saul's assault;
as shepherd boy and youth, he lives content,
and yet, when king, he lives for God's exalt.

Author: Carol Meeks

The Question That Was Never Asked

The misled biped
drove a car,
then rocket ship
from star to star
but still could not
locate the key
to one essential
mystery.

He stared through
giant telescopes
and climbed tall mountains
using ropes
and yet the secret
wasn't found
in outer space
or stony ground.

Modern science
replaced art
but couldn't find
the special part
though dainty tweezers
picked about
and peered within
and then without.

The shadow of the
absent thing
like missing hand
that fits the ring
eluded all
the brightest minds
who lost the fruit
but ate the rind.

What is the song
that has no words,
the shining wings
without a bird,
the oceans deep
and cobalt blue
that fit inside
a drop of dew?

To ask, my friend,
you first must feel
the love that made
both spokes and wheel
and understand
the world's a mirror.
You'll find the answer
everywhere.

Author: Nels Hanson

The Mourning Dove Recalls a Place

Dove-gray is blend
of blue and rose
and *cooing* is
as lovers know
what lovers do
when calm, at peace.

Before the days
of Rome or Greece
a single dove
bore olive leaves
from land to sea
with land's reprieve

to homesick Noah
at the mast
announcing all
rough seas were passed.
Doves' hush of wings
at evening tells

more softly, yet
as clear as bells
it's time the farmer
dropped the spade
as twilight fills
both field and shade.

When doves assume
the branch at dusk
in shadows cool
and murmurous
what loss, what ancient
hurt explains

the mourning dove's

forlorn refrain?
Sweet messenger
of longed-for rest,
you bear a wound
within your breast,

lament so sadly
of the night
dark trees grow
darker than they might.
The child at bedtime
hears your song,

a lullaby of things
gone wrong,
and learns from
half-remembered tones
of somewhere far
that once was home.

Author: Nels Hanson

Sir Knight

Little lord of my garden,
Your heart too fast, now faster
In breast of resplendent armor

As you string jade and golden filament
Between star jasmine and blue peppermint
And jasmine, in a blur,

Always arriving or just having been
To drink the bloom in a shiny whir—
I wonder

Toward what mysterious, Ultimate Flower
Are you flying
My knight, Sir Hummingbird?

Author: Nels Hanson

Born on a Sunday

"I was born on a Sunday,
A good child, she said.
God's own property
Stamped on my forehead,
In the womb I've been change
By water and by blood,
How, my heart did rejoiced
I have seen the Spirit as a dove.
I have felt His loving arms,
Sway me gently to His accord,
From the very start it seems,
I have been a friend of our Lord."

Author: Marchell Dyon Jefferson

Sevenling (A Daughter's Psalm)

A daughter's Psalm is to forgive our mothers,
To do this we must first love them,
For who they are, and not who we'd wish them to be,
Love them not as mothers, but women,
Fellows struggling like us,
From so many burdens laid upon the breast,
From not being heard.

Author: Marchell Dyon Jefferson

Victory

Running out of time
That's how I felt inside
My life - the ups and downs

Frustrated - I was losing my mind
Until one day I noticed I was
Completely off focus
Someone had stolen my view
Or perhaps I allowed them to
Something was missing
I had lots of tools but no screws
I asked to be set free
And fell
Demons were haunting me
I couldn't even sleep
This was the turning point in my life
I didn't think twice
I knew I had to seek Christ
Every night I would pray
To awake to more light
A change of appetite
More nourishment
Though I'm careful of the words I speak because
It's not an easy process
It's a lot to digest
I was blessed to hear angels sing
To help me through the struggles
Continuously I had to keep the faith
And keep my thoughts above the collar
My head high to the sky
Live for today and seek wisdom
To make it through tomorrow
Self-worth became my interest
And by far my only investment
Next to restore my sight
Appearing to have no way out like

Enter the Gateway

I'm stuck in this game but
Once I sat and thought about it
I realized we are all being played
Trapped in this earth's spin
Lost in emotions
Undertows and currents
Help came and though I was rescued I was also exhausted
With my head barely above water
I understood the message
But missed a valuable lesson
Unfortunately I couldn't swim
So here we go again
This time I'll pay more attention
Pick myself up dry myself off
Keep my eyes on the top
Increase my stamina open my mind
And push this grammar
Pray for peace and continue to resist the beast
Whether I'm on the hills or in the streets

Remember that words are blessings
Therefore never mistreat them
Regardless if you do
Or don't look like me
My visualization is on point
I adjust my focus to see everything I want
Aligning myself properly
Because I could have been history

Learning a valuable lesson
Framing everything
Living a life now that consists
Of more praise and forgiveness
More appreciation
Receiving more or less
I've learned knowing that
I've conquered
I've been promised

Every thought provides harmony
Every moment
Exhaling victory

Author: Michael Miller

They Laughed At Him

They laughed at Him
He hung His head
languishing
and as they scoffed
His body bled--drops
woeful drops they were
but He stayed true
and suffered through
completely in control.
I died with Him
and now He lives
thriving
at the Father's right hand
and I live in Him too.

Author: Mark Nenadov

Breath by Breath

Breath by breath
we draw more air
ascend and descend
life's creaky stairs
wondering
if there's a purpose
to show
for this gypsy life
and if someone knows,
controls, and cares.

We have no simple answers
that's so clear
for the pain and suffering
accumulating year by year
nor for the surprising beauty
that springs forth--from every corner
of the fallen earth.

We do have
an Answer
(not at all quaint)
wrapped up in the majestic One
who painted the Universe
the Life-Giver
all seeing
all knowing
in whom we live
and breathe
and have our being.

Author: Mark Nenadov

Evensong LXXX:
"Words in an Empty Shell"

The body laid to rest through passing time
Crumbles into dust, only bone left behind,
And should we examine the sleeping skeleton,
Would we be amazed to find
No bone where once was a tongue?
For such a mighty part of the body which
Stood so firm throughout its life,
Where are the remnants of this stick so sharp?
Did it pierce soil thick so that hand could drop a seed?

Lord, let not our tongues be like flint rock,
Should it meet another such stone
and clash together sending sparks into the air,
Igniting and setting on fire whatever
Good you have laid out ahead.

Teach us, O Savior, how to govern our hearts,
That love should bubble to the surface
And flow over our hot tongues,
Cooling its passion to destroy and hurt;
Help us, rather, to use our tongues
As a skillful sculptor might delicately chisel stone.

Author: Jesse Chandler

Evensong XIV:
"Watch on the Water"

High upon the mast, a body sits in a perch,
His watchful eyes trained across the water,
Charged with the duty to forewarn of danger,
For if we know stormy seas are on the rise,
We might prepare for the impending calamity;
Too often, though, our watch falls into slumber,
Our lack of devotion to the duty at hand
Catches us unawares, the storm is upon us, we cry out,
But our tiny voice is muffled by the crashing sea.

Furious waves lap bow and stern,
Fear grips the wheel, the rudder is unsteady,
A voice speaks out, "Quiet! Be still!"*
The wind lies down, the waves rest their torment,
The voice whispers, "Why are you so afraid?"**

Not oft do we question the miracle of ship
Buoyant upon the water,
No wonderment over the force pushing upon the sail,
Nor do we give a second thought to the stars
Above our head that guide us safely home,
Why, then, do we so often sink into our doubts?

Author: Jesse Chandler

---

*Mark 4:39
**Mark 4:40

Enter the Gateway

About the Authors:

(in alphabetical order by last name)

Cathy Baker is an award-winning poet who delights in observing God at work in the nuances of life, and sharing those observations through writing, journaling, and blogging. She and her husband Brian live in South Carolina with their answer to the empty-nest syndrome—a pampered pooch named Rupert. Visit Cathy's blog at www.cathybaker.org.

Jane Blanchard divides her time between Augusta and St. Simon's Island, Georgia. Her poetry has recently appeared in *Caveat Lector*, *James Dickey Review*, *Pearl*, *Pembroke Magazine*, *REAL*, *RiverSedge*, *Stone Voices*, and *The Vehicle*.

Jesse Chandler Jesse Chandler makes his home just outside of Richmond, Virginia. His Evensong poems have appeared in *Advent with Nurture Ministries*, *National Poetry Review*, and *The Bible Advocate*. He hopes to one day publish all the Evensongs into a book of daily devotion.

Carol Meeks is the 2011 Oklahoma Senior Poet Laureate at "Amy Kitchener's Angel Wings Contest." Meeks was the 2004, 2005, and 2007, NEW MEXICO SENIOR POET LAUREATE at the same contest. Meeks' poems have been placed in Writer's Digest top 100. Meeks has also received Honorable Mentions at Bylines, won contests in National State Poetry Society Contests, and published at *Poet's Forum*, *Potpourri* and *Red Ink*, among other small magazines. Meeks holds memberships in BARDS OF A FEATHER, NFSPS, Poetry Society of Oklahoma, High Prairie Poets Chapter of NMSPS, and chaired the committee for the bi-monthly contests held by High Prairie Poets.

Lisbon Chigwenjere is a young poet from Harare, Zimbabwe.

Nels Hanson has worked as a farmer, teacher, and contract writer/editor. He graduated from UC Santa Cruz and the U of Montana and his fiction received the San Francisco Foundation's James D. Phelan Award. His stories have appeared in *Antioch Review*, *Texas Review*, *Black Warrior Review*, *Southeast Review*, *Montreal Review*, and other journals. "Now the River's in You," a

Enter the Gateway

2010 story which appeared in Ruminate Magazine, was nominated for a Pushcart Prize, and "No One Can Find Us," which was published in *Ray's Road Review*, has been nominated for the 2012 Pushcart Prizes. His poems have appeared in *Poetry Porch*, *Red Booth Review*, *Meadowlands Review*, *Emerge Literary Journal*, and other magazines.

Richard Hartwell is a retired middle school English teacher living in Southern California. He has been previously published in: *The Cortland Review*, *Midwest Literary Review*, *Birmingham Arts Journal*, and several others.

Makeba Jackson is a poet currently living in Tampa, Florida with her husband and daughter.

Marchell Dyon Jefferson is from Chicago, Illinois. She has taken various poetry workshops; she is currently working on her first chapbook. Her work has appeared in *Ouroboros Review*, *WestWard Quarterly*, *Lily Review*, and Corner Club Press.

Erren Geraud Kelly is a poet based in Chicago. Kelly has been writing for 21 years and has been published in over three dozen publications in print and online including such publications as *Hiram Poetry Review*, *Mudfish*, *Poetry Magazine* (online) and other publications. Kelly's most recent literary work appeared in "In Our Own Words," a Generation X poetry anthology; Kelly was also published in other anthologies such as "Fertile Ground", "Beyond The Frontier" and other anthologies. Kelly is also the author of the chapbook "Disturbing The Peace," on Night Ballet Press. Kelly received a B.A. in English-Creative Writing from Louisiana State University in Baton Rouge

Thomas Koron was born in Grand Rapids, Michigan on May 19, 1977. He has attended Grand Rapids Community College, Aquinas College and Western Michigan University. He remains active in Grand Rapids as a writer, composer and performer.

Mark Nenadov lives in Essex, Ontario, Canada with his lovely wife and their baby daughter. Mark's poems have appeared in publications such as *Wilderness House Literary Review*, *WestWard Quarterly*, Northern Michigan University's *The Lightkeeper*, *Northern Cardinal Review*, *Calvary Cross*, and *Pif Magazine*. See http://www.marknenadov.com for more details.

Michael Miller is a poet born in Hamlet, North Carolina currently residing in Spartanburg, South Carolina. Miller writes poetry songs and short stories by occasion. Miller has also attended spoken word and poetry workshops.

David Schildroth has been reading and writing fiction and poetry for as long as he can remember.

Oneal Walters is a Toronto poet and the author of two poetry books. Find out more at www.onealwalters.com

Audrey Williams earned her MFA from Chicago State University. Her work has appeared in *The Alchemist Review* (flash fiction), an Honorable Mention from *ByLine Magazine* (novel excerpt), *Bewildering Stories* Website (short story), a short story in *African American Review* and a short story published by Sleepytown Press are forthcoming. She lives with Danielle, Chris, Jeremy, and Malik.

About the Publisher

TL Publishing Group is based out of Tampa, Florida. *Enter the Gateway* is the first poetry anthology published under Gateway Literature, an imprint of TL Publishing Group. Gateway Literature books provide readers with inspirational and uplifting poetry.

To learn more, please visit their website.

http://torridliterature.com

www.ingramcontent.com/pod-product-compliance
Lightning Source LLC
Chambersburg PA
CBHW060721030426
42337CB00017B/2958